Richard Claverhouse Jebb

The Work of the Universities for the Nation Past and Present

The inaugural lecture delivered at the Guildhall, Cambridge, on Saturday,

July 29, 1893

Richard Claverhouse Jebb

The Work of the Universities for the Nation Past and Present
The inaugural lecture delivered at the Guildhall, Cambridge, on Saturday, July 29, 1893

ISBN/EAN: 9783337035891

Printed in Europe, USA, Canada, Australia, Japan

Cover: Foto ©ninafisch / pixelio.de

More available books at **www.hansebooks.com**

𝕮𝖆𝖒𝖇𝖗𝖎𝖉𝖌𝖊 𝖀𝖓𝖎𝖛𝖊𝖗𝖘𝖎𝖙𝖞 𝕷𝖔𝖈𝖆𝖑 𝕷𝖊𝖈𝖙𝖚𝖗𝖊𝖘.

FOURTH SUMMER MEETING.

THE

WORK OF THE UNIVERSITIES

FOR THE NATION

PAST AND PRESENT

*THE INAUGURAL LECTURE
DELIVERED AT THE GUILDHALL, CAMBRIDGE
ON SATURDAY JULY 29 1893*

BY

R. C. JEBB, Litt.D. M.P.

REGIUS PROFESSOR OF GREEK AND FELLOW OF TRINITY COLLEGE

CAMBRIDGE:
AT THE UNIVERSITY PRESS.

1893

THE WORK OF THE UNIVERSITIES FOR THE NATION, PAST AND PRESENT.

This meeting, to which the University welcomes her visitors, not as strangers or aliens, but as members of a body united to her by common studies and sympathies, is a visible expression of that change which, during the last thirty years, has been passing over the relations between the ancient Universities of England and the country. They are no longer content to be only, in the strict sense of the phrase, seats of learning ; they now desire to be

J.   I

also mother-cities of intellectual colonies, and to spread the influence of their teaching throughout the land. It is indeed instructive to contrast this impulse with that feeling with which we meet in earlier ages, that any addition to the number of centres at which a higher education could be obtained was a menace to academic monopoly. In mediaeval times, when a body of Cambridge students withdrew to Northampton, Henry III., who had at first regarded the movement as likely to benefit the town to which they went, was presently induced to condemn it, as an infringement of privilege elsewhere ; and when Oxford students migrated to Stamford, they were peremptorily recalled by Edward III. In the days of the Commonwealth, the Master of Caius College, William Dell, proposed that the studies of

Oxford and Cambridge should be established also in the large towns of the west and north : the scheme was rejected, however, for a reason which, though valid at the time, was precisely opposite to that which in our own day has recommended University Extension ; it was held that such a measure would tend to diminish the influence of the Universities. The modern developments of railway travelling were necessary to render Extension, as we understand it, even possible ; but, before the opportunity could be used, something more vital was required,—the rise of a new spirit.

And this suggests that it may be not uninteresting to consider how far, and in what sense, that spirit is new ; what, in the past, has been the attitude of the Universities towards the nation ; and how far, at different periods, they have performed a national work. This is the subject with which I shall attempt, however slightly and imperfectly, to deal. It is scarcely necessary to observe that the sketch must be confined to salient points.

Rise of Universities in Europe.

The Universities of Europe sprang from a spontaneous and enthusiastic desire for knowledge. During the dark ages, from the fall of the Western Empire to the eleventh century, such education as existed was given in the schools attached to monasteries and cathedrals. Though some outlines of pagan literature were preserved, the subjects taught were mainly such as formed a direct preparation for the calling of the priest or the monk. Towards the end of this period, new studies began to press for recognition, partly through the stimulus given to Europe by contact with the more civilised East, a result to which the Crusades contributed. The practical studies of Medicine and of Law became more extended. The rudiments of physical science, and some branches of Mathematics, came more clearly into view. At the beginning of the twelfth century, the study of Dialectic, based on parts of the Aristotelian Logic, received a notable impulse. Its claim rested not only on its intrinsic value as a mental discipline, but upon its assumed relation to Theology. A belief was diffused, which some famous controversies of the time had strengthened, that spiritual truth could not be rightly apprehended except through certain forms of reasoning. This conception was the basis of what was afterwards known as the scholastic philosophy. Scholasticism began by dealing with certain problems of the The scholastic philosophy.

Aristotelian Logic (or what passed for such), and then applied its processes to Theology. The task which it ultimately undertook was that of reconciling the doctrines of the Church with human reason. This explains why, in the middle age, Dialectic was regarded as the paramount science, the highest which could engage man's intellect; since it was not only the handmaid of Theology, but in a certain sense the key to it.

The question now was, where could these new subjects be adequately studied? The ordinary range of instruction in the monastic and cathedral schools was too narrow to admit them. A few religious houses there were, doubtless, in which churchmen of exceptional gifts and attainments responded in some measure to the new desire; but these were inadequate to satisfy the wants of the age. Associations began to be formed, specially devoted to purposes of study. Such an association was commonly designated by one of two names ; *Studium Generale*, meaning a place *Studium Generale and Universitas.* of study not merely local, but open to all comers ; or *Universitas*, a corporation or guild, implying that teachers and learners formed a definitely incorporated body. The term *Universitas* being a general one, this special sense of it was defined by some addition ; we find such phrases as *Universitas Magistrorum et scholarium*, a corporation of masters and scholars ; or *Universitas literaria*. It was not probably till the close of the fourteenth century that the word *Universitas* came to be commonly used alone, in the sense of 'University.'

The earliest example of such a body dates from a time antecedent to the general awakening of the European mind, and is associated with the most indispensable of the practical sciences. The school of Medicine at Salerno in Southern Italy can be traced to the ninth century. But the twelfth century is that in which the first great Universities of Europe take their rise. Two of these are respectively typical of different tendencies in the higher teach-

Paris. ing of the age. The University of Paris became the great school of Dialectic and Theology: it represents especially the desire for a general mental training, with

Bologna. a speculative bent. The University of Bologna, famous for the study of the civil and canon law, gave the foremost place to the idea of a professional training, with a definite practical aim.

The English Universities. Paris was the model upon which the English Universities were founded. Before the end of the twelfth century, Giraldus Cambrensis could describe Oxford as the place 'where the clergy in England chiefly flourished, and excelled in clerkly lore.' The earliest history of our own University is more obscure; but it, too, probably had its origin in the twelfth century, in connection with teaching carried on by the canons of the Church of St Giles; and in 1209 we hear of some students migrating from Oxford to Cambridge. But it is not until we come to the era of the earliest Cambridge Colleges that there is any full or clear light. Throughout the middle age, Oxford was the representative University of England; and not only that, but at one time the rival, and in some respects the superior, of Paris. There are, however, indications enough to show that the development of mediaeval Cambridge was following the same general course.

First period : from about 1216 to 1350 A.D.

.The first period which we may take in the history of the English Universities starts from the time when they begin to have a distinct influence on the national life,—viz., from the early part of the thirteenth century,—and goes down to about the middle of the fourteenth. It answers roughly to the reigns of Henry III. and the first two Edwards, with the first half or so of Edward III.'s. This was the golden age

Oxford.

of the scholastic philosophy. At this period Oxford produced a series of famous schoolmen, among whom Roger Bacon, Duns Scotus, and William of Occam are only some of the most prominent,—doctors celebrated throughout Christendom. Nor were the studies confined to scholasticism, though that was in the foreground ; all other knowledge that the age possessed was pursued with ardour. Never since, perhaps, has any seat of learning given proofs of a more eager or varied activity than is attested by this long succession of brilliant Oxonians, many of whom were Franciscans. At this time the English Universities represented the best intellect and the highest knowledge that existed in the country. All men who cared for mental cultivation at all looked to them as the centres of education. Their attractive power was the more widely felt because the Church then offered the most varied avenues to advancement in life; indeed, there was no other road to it, except a military career. Many of us, perhaps, when we look back upon the mediaeval University, might be apt to think that after all it had little but the name in

The Universities really national.

common with the University of to-day.
In one sense, of course, this is true. An
impassable gulf divides them in respect to
material surroundings, to aims and methods
of study, to the whole fabric of government
and society. But, if we revert to the idea
in which Universities had their origin, we
find that the English University of the
thirteenth century fulfilled the essence of it ;
it possessed the highest culture of the age ;
and it was recognised by the nation as the
exponent of that culture.

This position rested primarily on the
dominance of the scholastic philosophy,
which, in turn, presupposed the unity of
Christendom. It is no paradox to say
that, in the twelfth and thirteenth centuries,
it was necessary for a University to be inter-
national before it could be worthily national.
Its rank depended on the eminence of its

teachers in studies which were acknow-
ledged as paramount throughout Europe,
and which were pursued in the common
language of learning, the Latin. At Paris
this cosmopolitan character appears in the
four 'nations' of that University, the
French, the Norman, the Picard, and the
English. At Oxford and Cambridge there
were only two nations, representing respectively the North and the South of
England ; but we hear of students from
Paris migrating to both our Universities ;
and the number of foreign students, especially at Oxford, must at one time have been
considerable.

With the second half of the fourteenth
century, however, we enter upon a new
period of our academic annals, in the
course of which the attitude of the Universities towards the nation was gradually

From 1350
to 1500
A.D.

but profoundly changed.   This stage may
be roughly defined as extending from
about 1350 to 1500.

Decay of
Scholasti-
cism.   The first great fact which meets us
here is the incipient decay of the scholastic
philosophy.   It declined, not because any
formidable rival had appeared in the field
of intellectual interests, but because the
age was slowly coming to perceive that
scholasticism had failed in the sublime task
which had inspired the dreams of its youth-
ful ambition.   It had not succeeded in
reconciling the doctrines of the Church
with human reason.   The extraordinary
enthusiasm and devotion which it had so
long commanded sprang from the belief
that, in the domain of knowledge, this
philosophy was a sort of counterpart to
the Holy Roman Empire in the sphere of
government, and that, as the Emperor

was in the old phrase the 'advocate' of the
Church, so the cultivation of the intellect
reached its climax in those studies where
the Dialectic bequeathed by Greece became the secular arm of Theology. But
theologians from one point of view, and
logicians from another, came to see that
the alliance had broken down ; semi-mysti-
cism on the one part, inchoate scepticism
on the other, became the refuge of dis-
appointment. And, when the scholastic
philosophy was once separated from its
loftiest purpose, what was it ? An armoury
of slowly rusting weapons, which could no
more do service in the greatest of the
causes for which they had been elaborated.
The weary guardians of the armoury might
shift the places of those weapons on the
dusty walls, and make some show of
keeping them decently keen and bright ;

but they could not feel the joyous energy of the soldier who had sharpened and burnished them for battle.   Long afterwards, Erasmus expressed what the fourteenth century had already begun to feel, when, asking how Christendom was to set about converting Turks, he said—'Shall we put into their hands an Occam, a Durandus, a Scotus, a Gabriel, or an Alvarus ?   What will they think of us, when they hear of our perplexed subtleties about Instants, Formalities, Quiddities, and Relations?' Considered merely as an instrument of mental discipline, the scholastic philosophy had done good work for the age in which it arose ; it has left, indeed, an abiding mark on the language and the thought of Europe ; but it was now passing into a system of lifeless formulas and mechanical exercises.   Thus the Universities were

losing—slowly but surely—that which had once been their sovereign attraction. And at the same time they were denied an outlet for new activities. Wyclif's gallant struggle at Oxford was defeated. His death in 1384 marks a turning-point. Religious freedom was suppressed, but at the cost of intellectual life. The crusade against Lollardism introduced an age of torpor and sterility at the Universities. Indeed, the Latin philosophy was gradually silencing itself. And a decided divorce between the Universities and the nation was now setting in. The laity felt less interest in the paralysed studies of the academic schools, which were tending to become little more than clerical seminaries. The numbers of the students were dwindling. Already the study of Medicine was withdrawing to the large towns ; the study

J.

2

of Law was dropping off to the Inns of
Court.   It is also a significant circumstance
that the second half of the 14th century
coincides with an advance in the literary
use of the English language, as represented
by Chaucer and Gower, and by Wyclif
himself.   This fact does not in itself imply
any antagonism to the Universities, but it
reminds us that a national literature was
now growing which was independent of
their influence.

Rise of the
Colleges.

Thus far we have contemplated what
may be called the negative side of the
period from 1350 to 1500.   The Universities were beginning to lose their hold
upon the nation ; their old mental life
was failing.   But there is another side
to this period, and one which gives it a
strong claim upon our interest.   This
was the era at which the power of the

Colleges was slowly rising. Of our seventeen Cambridge Colleges, only one was founded before 1300, and only three were founded after 1550. At Oxford, three Colleges arose before 1300; and though a larger number of foundations than here came after 1550, still we may say that, at both Universities, the fourteenth and fifteenth centuries form the period during which the power of the Colleges was chiefly consolidated. The general intention of the earliest Colleges was that they should be boarding-houses, with a discipline so organised that the inmates should lead a studious and decorous life,—special provision being made for those who required pecuniary aid. Many Colleges were designed more especially for the secular clergy, as the monastic and mendicant orders were

2—2

already so amply endowed. We must remember that the multitude of students at a mediaeval university was a fluctuating and often turbulent mass. The great value of the Collegiate system, when it first came in, lay not so much in the pecuniary assistance which it gave, as in the security which it afforded for discipline and good order. It was an element of permanence and cohesion for the whole academic body. The teaching function, it may be added, did not belong to the original idea of a College, except in so far as the older residents might be expected to aid or guide the studies of the younger ; a College teaching-staff was a later development, due to the altered status of the University schools.   .

The new classical learning: While the Universities, as such, long continued to be identified with the mori-

bund scholasticism, the Colleges, from the
fifteenth century onwards, were more especially identified with the new learning,
—with the classical revival. At the
time of Wyclif's death, that revival was
passing, in Italy, through its earliest
phase, under the immediate followers of
Petrarch, who felt the new delight of
discovery. In the first half of the fifteenth century, the groups gathered
around Cosmo de' Medici at Florence,
or Nicholas V. at Rome, were busied
in arranging the discovered materials ;
and before 1500 criticism had been
carried further, chiefly by Italian societies
and academies. In due time this new its advent,
compared
humanism spread to England. But we with that
of scholas-
observe a striking difference between ticism.
the conditions under which this movement reached us, and those which had

surrounded the advent of its great pre-
decessor, the scholastic philosophy, in
the twelfth century. That philosophy
had hardly begun its course when, owing
to the intervention of the Dominicans
and Franciscans, it was enabled to advance
under the banners of the Church. No
equivalent patronage protected or en-
couraged the first endeavours of our
English humanists. It was not until the
middle of Henry VIII.'s reign that the
humanities began to enjoy the doubtful
advantage of official favour; and then
the classical muse might already have
responded—if only she had dared—in the
tone of Dr Johnson's reply to the tardy
civilities of Lord Chesterfield. The re-
stored classical learning was planted in
England by the enterprise and zeal of
a few individuals, such as that series of

Hellenists whom Oxford can show at the close of the fifteenth century,—Selling, Lilly, Grocyn, Latimer, Linacre ; such as Cambridge, again, produced in the immediately subsequent period,—Richard Croke, Thomas Smith, and that able scholar, whom Ascham and Milton commemorate, Sir John Cheke. The Colleges sheltered most of those who brought the new learning into England. These foundations afforded opportunities for private study,—and it must be recollected that the new learning, Greek especially, carried the suspicion of heresy ;—they also facilitated foreign travel, which was then almost indispensable for the purpose. But the classics, though the circle of those interested in them became continually larger, could not exercise such a widespread or popular influence as once belonged to the old mediaeval studies. ⌈ The strong-

The Col- holds of humanism, again, the Colleges,
leges.
—as their permanent character, their
wealth, and the ability of their adminis-
trators gradually made them predominant,
—represented an aristocratic or at least
oligarchic agency, engrafted upon the once
democratic existence of the mediaeval university.⌋ Thus, in the second half of
the fifteenth century, internal causes were
tending to detach the Universities from
the general life of the nation, while at
the same time the number of other interests
and careers was expanding.

Erasmus. The early years of the sixteenth century are made memorable for Cambridge
by the residence here of Erasmus, from
the end of 1510 to the end of 1513. In
his earlier stay at Oxford, he had enjoyed
most congenial and instructive friendships ;

but here, at least, he did some of his ripest
and hardest work,—kindling the minds of
disciples, too, who carried on the tradition.
It was in the old tower of Queens' College
that he completed a collation of the Greek
text of the New Testament; and four
years later his edition—the first ever published—appeared at Basle. It was in this
University, and in the years just after the
visit of Erasmus, that the Reformation had The Reformation.
its English birth. It was a time, too,
when Cambridge men were zealously con-
tinuing those classical studies in which
the Hellenists of Oxford had been
pioneers. It is interesting to recall what
Erasmus wrote in 1520 to Everard, the Cambridge
in 1520
Stadtholder of Holland: 'Theology is A.D.
flourishing at Paris and at Cambridge as
nowhere else; and why? Because they
are adapting themselves to the tendencies

of the age ; because the new studies, which
are ready, if need be, to storm an entrance,
are not repelled by them as foes, but received as welcome guests.' John Skelton
was even moved to satirise the zeal for
Greek which prevailed at Cambridge in
1521.

But this fair promise was too soon
overclouded. A time of unrest and anxiety
was at hand. Poverty and discontent,
legacies from the past century, were widespread in the land; the Church was
wealthy, and powerless to defend its wealth;
Danger of the Universities were identified, in the
the Uni-
versities. public eye, with the Church, and, like it,
were in danger of spoliation. Oxford and
Cambridge were glad to have Wolsey's
protection; and after his fall, it was of
vital moment to them to win the favour of
the king. The king did indeed stand

their friend : when courtiers urged that the Universities should be plundered, he declared that he judged no land in England better bestowed than that which was devoted to the uses of learning. But in return he exacted submission to his will. The visitation of the Universities by Thomas Cromwell's Commissioners took place in 1535, when the Royal Injunctions were issued. They imposed the acceptance of the royal supremacy, abolishing the lectures and degrees in the canon law. They prescribed the study of Latin and Greek, and of the Old and New Testaments, to the exclusion of the old scholastic text-books. These Injunctions may indeed be regarded as formally marking the fall of scholasticism. They constitute an official boundary-line between the mediaeval learning and the new.

Royal Injunctions of 1535.

But the reform failed to bear good fruit. During the years from 1535 to Mary's death in 1559 the Universities were at a low ebb. At first, no doubt, the level of their work seemed to be rising. But Henry had narrowly circumscribed their intellectual freedom; they were suffering from poverty; and they were distracted by all the fierce controversies of the time. A mischief of a new kind had also crept in. After the expulsion of the religious orders, youths of the richer classes began once more to frequent the Universities, as their parents had no longer to fear the influence of monk or friar. Thus in 1549 Latimer said, referring to Cambridge, 'There be none now but great men's sons in College, and their fathers look not to have them preachers.' Academic corruption followed. Roger Ascham says, 'Talent, learning,

poverty and discretion all went for nothing..., when interest, favour, and letters
from the great exerted their pressure
from without.' Perhaps the Universities
were never less truly national than in
those years.

Elizabeth's reign opened a new era. Elizabe-
than age
Not that it was a brilliant period in aca- (1559—
1603).
demic studies. With the partial exception
of Theology, no branch of learning was
really flourishing at the ancient seats.
However, a decided change came about in
the general position of the Universities.
For two centuries, they had been more or
less isolated ; and the internal forces which
shaped them had been mainly ecclesiastical.
These conditions were now sensibly modi-
fied. Elizabeth, whose gifts and attainments
disposed her to appear as a patroness of
letters, showed much favour to the Uni-

versities.   In the year of Shakespeare's
birth (1564) she made a visit of five days
to Cambridge, and not long afterwards
bestowed a like honour upon Oxford.   By
these and similar acts she increased the
social prestige of the Universities.   Now,
too, they came into closer contact with the
life of the capital.   In London there was a
world of letters which, though it received
many recruits from Oxford and Cambridge,
was by no means academic in character.
A stream of popular literature now began
to flow from London to the Universities.
Frequent intercourse sprang up between
University students and the town wits,
and was promoted by the fact that University men were continually passing into
the ranks of the Inns of Court.   It may
be conjectured that the results were not
altogether good for academic discipline ;

but there was some real gain in the literary impulse given to the Universities. It was also better that they should be drawn more into the currents of a wider and fuller life, even though those currents were sometimes turbid, than they should remain in isolation. Elizabeth's reign was a time in which the Universities were tending to acquire a certain character of exclusiveness,—not, indeed, in any very narrow sense, but relatively to the nation at large. On the other hand it was certainly a time when they resumed something of their old relations with a world larger and more varied than their own.

At the opening of the seventeenth century we find the Universities enjoying, under James I., a continuance of royal favour. But they were not prospering as seats of learning. Much as James relished

The 17th century.

theological disputations and College plays, his first object in regard to Oxford and Cambridge was that they should uphold the royal supremacy in matters of religious belief. Under all the Stuart monarchs the case was the same; the first thing asked of Oxford and Cambridge was that they should inculcate sound doctrines in Church and State : their condition in respect of learning was a secondary matter. In the Great Rebellion both the Universities were royalist; and the Barebones Parliament once discussed the propriety of suppressing them altogether. Milder counsels prevailed, and under the Protectorate it was resolved that 'the Universities and schools shall be so countenanced and reformed as that they may become the nurseries of piety and learning.' Shortly afterwards, however, a more rigorous plan was mooted,—viz., that the number of Colleges in each University should be cut down to three, answering respectively to the faculties of Divinity, Law, and Physic. The Restoration quickly averted that peril; and the Revolution, in its turn, delivered the Universities from those strained exercises of royal prerogative in which the last two Stuart kings occasionally indulged. Certainly the seventeenth century was not one in which it could be expected that the average level of academic life should be a high one. And yet, throughout that century, the two old seats of learning were producing a long series of men whose intellectual achievements in various fields are among the chief glories of England. It may be hard to say what exact share of credit is due, in any of these cases, to the *Alma*

Mater; but it is reasonable to believe that in no instance can her influence have been wholly sterile. Cambridge can point to such names as those of Bacon, William Harvey, Milton, Barrow, Newton, Bentley; then there are the Oxford and Cambridge divines who bore part in the Authorised Version of the Bible, or helped to build up the standard Anglican theology; the Oxford group who founded the Royal Society; the Cambridge Platonists, who sought, in a spirit very different from that of the schoolmen, to reconcile religion with philosophy and science, to soften the strife of sects, and to bring out the essential things of Christianity. When one looks back on that century as a whole,— on the turmoils and contrasts of its outer life, and on the results of its mental activity,—one is inclined to apply the old

Greek saying to our academic common-wealths ; ' It is not the walls that make the city, but the men.'

The age which came next has usually been regarded as that in which the English Universities were least alive to their national duties and responsibilities. I shall not attempt to offer a defence for the academic shortcomings of the eighteenth century. But, if the censure is not to be too sweeping, it is well to observe certain points. First—we should remember that those studies which Universities seek to foster cannot really thrive unless they are animated by at least some touch of ardour, some spark of a generous enthusiasm. They are sensitive to the atmosphere about them, and are apt to be chilled by a surrounding apathy. The eighteenth century, correct, judicious, ob-

The 18th century.

3—2

servant of measure and obedient to
common sense, gave little encourage-
ment to large aspirations or lofty ideals.
These, however, are the breath of life
to young students, and most of all to
the best. Never, perhaps, did scholars
work with greater intensity than the great
schoolmen of the thirteenth century ;—
Duns Scotus, for instance, dying, it is
said, at thirty-four, left the equivalent of
thirteen printed folios ;—and they could
do so, because the ideal before them was
so grand. The eighteenth century was in
this respect at the opposite pole from
the thirteenth. There was little in it to
feed the sacred fire. If the Universities
were torpid, their fault was at least so far
the less, that they were breathing an
unfavourable air. In the next place, it
should be noted that the torpor was not

unbroken or universal. Like the heroes in
the battles of the Iliad, the two Universities have their respective moments of pre-
eminence ; and in regard to the eighteenth
century, an impartial inquirer will conclude,
I think, that Cambridge, though very far
from blameless, held some advantage.
There were two principal reasons for this.
First, that century opened here with a
period during which Bentley and Newton
were giving a powerful impulse to studies
old and new. Chairs of Astronomy, A-
natomy, Geology, and Botany were founded
between 1702 and 1727. Secondly, there
was at least one study, that of Mathematics,
which was pursued here with real industry
and success during at least the second
half of the century ; when a great improvement was also effected in the tests of
mathematical attainment. Yet it is not to

be denied that, on the whole, both Universities then fell far short of any standard
which could be deemed worthy of their
position ; nor is it a sufficient plea that,
during the eighteenth century, they can
claim so many sons distinguished in
letters, science, or active careers.

Early part
of this cen-
tury.
Institutions are seldom at their worst
when the outcry against them is loudest.
Before public opinion reaches the point
which threatens interference from without,
conscience and prudence usually make
themselves heard within. During the first
third of this century, steps were taken at
both the Universities to improve the quality
and enlarge the scope of their work ; and
if these steps did not go very far, at least
they were laudable in their way. Meanwhile
the voice of censure, which had been almost
silent in the eighteenth century, became

more importunate. Its tone was such as
we find in these words of Dugald Stewart,
which were pointed especially at the English
Universities :—' The academical establish-
ments of some parts of Europe,' he said,
' are not without their use to the historian
of the human mind. Immovably moored
to the same station by the strength of their
cables and the weight of their anchors, they
enable him to measure the rapidity of the
current by which the rest of mankind is
borne along.' The time of the first Reform The demand for
Bill is that at which the unpopularity of reform.
Oxford and Cambridge began to be general.
In a series of articles contributed to the
' Edinburgh Review,' Sir William Hamilton
framed an indictment against them which
attracted much attention. Within the
Universities themselves, the more active
minds were fully alive to the necessity for

further improvement. Foremost among
these was Adam Sedgwick, whose ' Dis-
course on the Studies of the University of
Cambridge' appeared in 1833. A Cambridge graduate who published in 1836 a
letter[1] on the 'Condition, Abuses, and
Capabilities of the National Universities,'
remarks that, if he ventures to point out
defects, he will be asked 'whether he wishes
that our youth should be better educated
than Bacon, Locke, and Newton'; but he
makes it clear that his own opinions were
shared by many Cambridge residents. To
foreign observers the peril of our academic
situation was equally manifest. Huber, a
Professor at Marburg, published his History
of the English Universities in 1839. He
was a lenient judge; sometimes even too

[1] It will be found in a volume of 'Tracts' in the
University Library, BB. 26, 33.

lenient. But he recognises the existence
of a hostile feeling against Oxford and
Cambridge, which is proclaimed, he says,
'in every variety of tone and manner, and
from the most different quarters.'

Let us note the causes of this feeling. The two
chief de-
First, there had been, since the seventeenth fects.
century, a great expansion in science and
literature, with which the Universities had
not kept pace. They no longer adequately
represented the knowledge of the age, or
the best intellect of the nation. Secondly,
the instruction which they did give—and
in some subjects it was better than it had
ever been before—was virtually limited to
certain classes of society, defined partly by
wealth, and partly by religious opinion.
That moment was the earliest at which it
had become apparent to the country at
large that, in both these senses, the Uni-

versities failed to be national.   And the
perception was quickened by the new
democratic tendencies.

It is curious to observe what Huber
—a friendly critic—regarded as the one
tenable ground of defence.   He says, in
effect : 'The end for which the English
Universities have long existed has not
been to form learned men, or able professional men, or State officials, as our
German Universities do ; it has been to
produce that first and most distinctive
flower of English national life, an English
gentleman ; a product to which we on the
Continent have nothing really similar ; the
nearest approach to it is a Castilian *cabal-
lero.*'   No doubt there were many people in
England—men inspired with a lofty idea
of what a University ought to be—who,
when they read those words of the German

historian, felt in them a severe, though unconscious, irony. And yet, if we wish to be quite just to the work which the Universities did for the nation from 1600 to 1850, we are bound to recognise the how far true. element of truth which Huber's remark contains. Seats of education, which for centuries have existed in the midst of a vigorous people, can never be colourless embodiments of a desire for knowledge ; they are necessarily influenced, in different ways at different periods, by the national genius of that people. And it belongs to Bent of the English the genius of the English people—in genius. modern days at any rate—to value character more than intellect, and ability more than learning. Hence there have long been currents of influence, bearing on the Universities from outside, which have tended to a sort of compromise between the function proper to a University and that function of social education which can also be performed by a good regiment, or by any other society in which young men act and re-act upon each other under the two-fold sway of a public opinion controlled by themselves and a discipline above them. When allowance has been made for all shortcomings, it must be granted that the English Universities have not only rendered great services to learning and science, but have also done good work for the nation by forming characters in which at least some measure of liberal education has been combined with manliness.

That, however, is no longer the only ground upon which they can claim to be national. The successive reforms which Reforms since 1850. have been accomplished since 1850 have been directed to remedying or mitigating the two principal defects, narrowness of study, and narrowness of social operation. The range of studies has been immensely enlarged ; and though much remains to be done, it may be said of both Universities that at no previous time have they been the seats of intellectual work at once so highly organised and so varied. Within the last twenty-five years, too, their doors have been opened to whole classes of the community against which they were once closed.

But the historian of the future will see something still more distinctive of our time in the spirit which has moved the Universities to take up a new position in regard to national education beyond their own precincts. In the course of the thirty-five years since the Local Examinations were established, the Universities have done much

Attitude towards national education.

Local Examinations.

towards elevating and organising secondary education in the schools concerned, and have thus contributed something, at least, towards supplying what is still the chief need in our educational system.   Larger and more fruitful still has been the working of that later but essentially kindred movement which, twenty years ago, this University, moved by Mr James Stuart, had the honour of initiating, and which both the old Universities, in alliance with younger but vigorous agencies, are now prosecuting in generous emulation.   To an audience such as this, comprising many of those whose untiring energy and distinguished ability have made University Extension what it is—comprising, as it also does, a yet larger number of those who have tasted the benefits of the movement—it is superfluous to speak in detail of conditions, methods, and results

The Extension movement.

with which none are so intimately acquainted as themselves. Looking at the movement in its broad aspects, we see that the missionary enterprise of the Universities is imparting a new stimulus to the country, and is labouring to satisfy the demand which has been recognised or created. No task can be more patriotic than that of knitting the whole community together by common mental associations and enjoyments. 'Surely as Nature createth brotherhood in families,' said Bacon, 'so in like manner there cannot but be fraternity in learning and illuminations.' But the benefits are not all upon one side. If the Universities give, they also receive. Many of their ablest men, the leaders and workers in this movement, testify that they have learned lessons which could have been acquired in no other way. The Universities themselves, as we venture to hope, are gradually winning a place in the affections of the country which must needs be the best of incentives to good work.

The present need. The great object now is to place University Extension on a more permanent and systematic basis. The difficulty is simply want of funds. The Universities, as such, are far from rich, relatively to the claims upon them ; and if farther financial aid is to come from an academic source, it is to be looked for rather in the following of that admirable example which has been set by more than one College. The case for aid from the State is a strong one, and has been stated more than once with a force to which nothing can be added. It has been pointed out that the State spends three millions a year on Elementary Education, and that a small grant

—say £5000 a year—to University Extension,—a grant which might in the first instance be temporary and tentative,— would greatly increase the value of the return which the country obtains for the larger expenditure. Elementary instruction, unless crowned by something higher, is not only barren, but may even be dangerous. It is not well to teach our democracy to read, unless we also teach it to think. The County Councils' grants go at present to one side of the movement only, —the technical and scientific; and, far from weakening the argument for some further State aid, they really strengthen it. Such thoughts naturally occur to the mind at such a gathering as this; but no uncertainty which may hang over the future can diminish the feelings of gratification at past success, and of good augury for fur-

J.   4

ther development, which such an occasion is fitted to inspire.

In conclusion, I would only venture to express the earnest hope that this summer meeting may prove no unworthy successor, in every benefit and enjoyment which such an experience can afford, to the meetings which have preceded it ; and that our visitors, whom the University so warmly welcomes, may find here, in the temporary home of their studies, something of that mysterious influence which nowhere does its spiriting more gently than in a venerable seat of learning,—the genius of the place. True it is that in these ancient courts and halls, in the cloisters and the gardens, the charm which one feels is inseparably blended with a certain strain of melancholy. How often, in the long course of the centuries, have these haunts been associated, not only with the efforts which triumphed and the labours which bore lasting fruit, but also with the lost causes and the impossible loyalties, with the theories which were overthrown, with the visions which faded, with the brave and patient endeavours which ended in failure and defeat! Nevertheless, this place speaks to us of a corporate intellectual life which has been continuous; not always, indeed, free from the incubus of superstition or the heavy hand of external despotism; not always exempt from a depressing lethargy within; yet always preserving some secret spring of recuperative vigour, and thus linking the present with the past by a tradition which has in a great measure run parallel with the fortunes of England. And now, when these scenes, so dear to those whose life is passed among them, are animated by the presence of visitors who have already experienced the influences which Cambridge fosters, there is no one here who will not feel that the familiar features of our old academic home have a light upon them which our fathers never saw,—the light kindled by this new and living sympathy between the Universities and the nation.

CAMBRIDGE: PRINTED BY C. J. CLAY, M.A. & SONS, AT THE UNIVERSITY PRESS.

www.ingramcontent.com/pod-product-compliance
Lightning Source LLC
Chambersburg PA
CBHW022040080426
42733CB00007B/912